LOSSLESS

LOSSLESS

poetry by
Matthew Tierney

Coach House Books, Toronto

first edition

Published with the generous assistance of the Canada Council for the Arts and the Ontario Arts Council. Coach House Books also acknowledges the support of the Government of Canada through the Canada Book Fund and the Government of Ontario through the Ontario Book Publishing Tax Credit.

LIBRARY AND ARCHIVES CANADA CATALOGUING IN PUBLICATION

Title: Lossless / poetry by Matthew Tierney.
Names: Tierney, Matthew, author.
Identifiers: Canadiana (print) 20240287282 | Canadiana (ebook) 20240287312 | ISBN 9781552454794 (softcover) | ISBN 9781770568068 (PDF) | ISBN 9781770568051 (EPUB)
Subjects: LCGFT: Poetry.
Classification: LCC PS8589.I42 L677 2024 | DDC C811/.6—dc23

Lossless is available as an ebook: ISBN 978 1 77056 805 1 (EPUB), 978 1 77056 806 8 (PDF)

for Charmaine & August

is it?

Isn't it?

   The fog lifted.

It was early spring, still.

— CARL PHILLIPS

01

THEN THE FLOODLIGHTS WHILE SKATING AT MONARCH PARK

Outdoor rink a turret / to which
    the distant CN Tower
    signals imperative, benevolence. Mid-
afternoon laterals the sun: Augie

    refuses to agree
    he's cold. Hours seep into strata.

My son, I'm humbled
by your effort. To breach / the impregnable, hold

    in mind compossible paths
        from causal whole. Our lean & hew
        makes on the ice sheet a dendri-
    form. The moment's covenant, you

        with arms thrown back, helmet down –
        knight-errant – swiftly, for kingdom.

MOUNT SINAI FERTILITY AT ITS NEW LOCATION

Three-star-hotel lobby or rescaled
departure lounge. A pot-lit *maybe*.

A pair decouples at reception, bi-
    nomials factored. One
disappears, one waits.

Beneath all, the dark trickle
    no one hears, comfy seats beside me
    and across / simultaneously
occupied & unclaimed, seven years

    turning as-advertised to
        as is. *Flip flip flip*
    goes the unsayable, the do-overs.

A decaying note asks of itself
its origins in a material universe.

SIX YEARS OLD ON A SOLO JOURNEY TO BUY CANDY

This many minutes in wet jacket & toque,
     I feel in the store's yellow light
     the slickness, the insistence,
of undertow. Curve of road along

     which I walked alone / now forgotten.
          Periphery frays
          beyond aisles & register:
     still further, numbers wink, deep set

          in nightfelt. Silver & copper
               fleets on my palm, counter trays
          steadfast. Choice, I choose you.

Hands full, I lose myself, head
     for the door. The shop owner, hard as rain:
'Hey you, you haven't paid.'

A BONEHEADED MOVE I RELIVE FOR YEARS

Thought experiments on thought:
    Sunday, final match, endgame, pawns,
kings. Time trouble delineates table & crowd like a

    light shaft from Valhalla
        while across the board Einstein
    double-checks twin clocks …

Purse on the line, my opponent, me,
greybeard & tweener.

Canals angle through event space:
    frisson corners & compels
my moves. I levitate, see the win, promptly

    fumble the tempo.
        Ungraspable, unfathomable, purest of
mates. I'm inconsolable. *Scene.*

WHAT WE TALKED ABOUT IN GRADE 10 WAITING AFTER SCHOOL AT THE MORNINGSIDE TTC STOP

is mostly lost to lift: a butterfly knife
    untwists to nick its
flightpath. The architectonic

    brain disintegrates.
        Empirical I is
        a poor host, porous, a sow thistle
    blown off course into

        a neighbour universe. I close my eyes to
        the gold hilt. Over the crest the bus.

The sidewalk mass shapeshifts, baggy,
    the infectious lot of us
shot by time's arrow.

You shall wilt before the end, said no one
to no one's friend.

As bass line, malingerer, I run
    a finger in a fingerless glove over
a smooth slab, adrift through / the stelae.

A thought, set vertical.
    An aria projectile, all
trajectory.

Nothing lies like a grid.

From above, foreign chatter.
    A flock of birds into the blue –
a cardiogram shattered. Figure

    uncarved within the concrete:
        transcend matter, unlove the
      blackness you're in.
    Because beckons.

VISITING THE HOUSE BEFORE SHE DIED AND IT BECAME OURS

Wallpaper a green green ... cardamom?
    Old-forest canopy at midday?
    An organic host for some
fleur-de-lis-inspired flourish.

You gave the penny to the angel, the lever
    made her nod – through tiny bronze
collection-box slot, into the dark,

    I pictured each / a pebble
    falling on a mountaintop.

Great Nana, you let me work out the base's
    stopper to restock
    while adults with adult faces
watched. Copper dust suspended like

    faith. Electrostatic build-up in the keep. / Repeat.

FROM THE FERRY DECK ON OUR VACATION FROM TRYING

The Baltic Sea in February.

Midnight-blue ice
     cages an auroral flicker:
     deep-sea diamondback, cresting:
tartan scarf knitted

          to the Finnish shore. / Metaphor
               carries us, wraps tight
          the blister. A flattened soul is one

               that tinkers like an automaton
                    while Centauri thunders
               to the horde. Soon soothes. Ribboned

                    with expanse, excitable, we project ourselves:
                         dropped onboard into a somehow
                    like Helsinki.

WE ARE TOLD THERE IS NO LONGER A HEARTBEAT

Eggshell blue. The ER doctor
    tugs the curtain closed. The shiver
rings tight around us.

Lack

    occurs, a big bang that'll
        generate a life force,
        day after day expanding. At its centre,
    forever weighted, full-throated, you.

Intake & sorrow. A bleb
    on the glass furrow refracting
    the sun's tentacled rays, prismatic fan
cast on memory-palace inlay.

O surprise.
O liquidity.

AS OLDEST I WAS LATE TO EVERYTHING

Wakeful: a surface ripple here, there:
    two brothers in the room's bunk
    asleep / on a moonlit ride. In the side twin
    I've jacked off, mimicking a crude gesture
seen in *Christine*.

Curtainless, phosphorus night-grey
    for None to see
    my spirit numbness. No sperm, a drip of se-
men. Invisible

    flame, Catholic boy licked by
    Stephen's demon. Hands, idle. *Fiat nox.*

All creation threads
    springcreak, crosshatch & flicker into that
which next transpires.

THE LINING IN THE COFFIN AT THE VIEWING

Shiny satin folds, like a
    sonnet's volta. Undulation
a continuum. Bodies / bode ill,

        erupt from mineral. How I at times slip
            a fingerpad on the nail nubbin
            protruding from my tibia:
        titanium: biocompatible.

We are made of effort, not will.

Grandma, I have noticed people
    who re-situate plants to sills
    are unlike me. Yet I'll steal an iota
from the noiseless sun,

        glossy and recital ready.
        The best of us, down on down.

ON HEARING YOUR BIRTH MOTHER CHOSE US TO ADOPT YOU

Memory of pain / is not pain.
    The clearing, a circle of
embrace & resistance.

Along its perimeter
    wavelengths crackle, like a telegraph key
taking on the Atlantic.

You were known of
    before known.
        We, fearful of love, the unforeseen
        an impulse-blown field in shards
        at our feet: air a live circuit:
    each breath first arrival then dust-
torn sigh of the circus, pulling out of town –

    we, bless us, held on.

At 4 p.m.: an African savanna / plated
behind Nana's bungalow, Marmora.

God or apophenia
    restocked my ambit each day with
    dupable praying mantises, jam-jar-fodder
    grasshoppers. One rock, two rocks, twig.
Mercy-pierced tin lid.

Sashes of goldenrod and tallgrass
    brushed by an August
    breeze. The end half of the half-acre
    a flotilla of maple, cedar, beech
that prefigured a path ...

Once round then leap! Its apex
a gift more generous than strength.

HOMEWARD AFTER A DAY OF HIGHER LEARNING

Slipshod elongated onboarding of a
    north-end afternoon: the York Mills 95A
    unsnaps its door, hydraulic hiss
dissociating hippo from campus.

Cogito hiccups
    beachballing
thought to ego, ego to act. / Whosoever is is

    on autopilot. *Quod erat demonstrandum*
        instantiates subjects
        from consequence & fidget.
    An other, invariant, he

        conjures agency. He, on occasion,
        in semesters subsequent, he & I

        will collide.

HER PARENTS GOT ME A SUMMER JOB PAINTING SCHOOLS WITH THE SAVED

Crushed velvet wad inside my skull,
    hour hand creeps into a.m., her parents
in bed asleep but fully aware

    their Lord and Saviour is awake.

Interminable / propagation:
    macro crackle in the sound stage
    of postcoital-spiked den.
MuchMusic on loop, it's 'Oh Girl'

    sung by Paul Young / again. Again
        sleep's an illicit drug,
        melatonin swells the honeycombs:
    hi-gloss varsity-blue metal door-

    frames I walk arm in arm with her
    through & through & through.

AUGUST AT ONE-AND-A-HALF ON THE DON VALLEY BRICK WORKS TRAIL

Lying on the dock by the lily pads'
    penitential bloat. Aliens prep
aerials, float in on

    the breeze. The tingle we feel / vestigial,
        cued by the evergreen monocline,
        a shade too tropical
    for northern autumn.

The clinamen: a turtle,
    its shell gradient just / distinguishable
    from murk. Stagnant pond, burps of
Precambrian glue.

Kids congregate.
    Peering through slats, you: your bundle
of patience.

LEFT TO MY OWN DEVICES WITH MY YOUNG FATHER

The track gravel a coarse grain, a smokeblack
    materialization of
    Dickensian longing & fate. / Dad
would train for his thirties, I'd

    watch, jog three-quarter laps, finger
        to ribbons the blades of grass
        beside our Adidas gym bag, its red sash
    slashing world's-edge blue.

No thought given to
    the polyrhythm. Tensile strings tune
    a supersensible pitch: somewhere
in that field, phantasy turns

    a dog into
    dog-with-frisbee, midair.

GRANDMA BO'S FARM FOR A SPELL IN SEPTEMBER

Lawn tractor tops out
    at a brisk walk, stitches
    the hem of cedar stand, then / reloads
for the east acre's flock of geese.

On the trailer's unsecured
    plastic folding chair, my sore ass.
    Pain is an engine that goes & goes,
    what-what-what resounding afield
as an amplitude flux.

Beside me Augie's laughter a light cone, advancing.
    Hammer & tongs jar the collective: waddles, honks
from the rearguard ...

On notice, aren't we always.
All at once the geese, up toward.

COINCIDENT WITH '52ND STREET' PLAYING IN MY WALKMAN

Hustling off the GO. Untucked
    summer. Behold the seasonal, spindle-
    legged, glassy-eyed employee.
I lope toward Ontairy-airy-airy-o

Place while
    from Exhibition Stadium speakers
    Billy Joel's 'Zanzibar'
ricochets around 50,000 empty seats –

    morning's deepest cut. The deadlands contain
        echo and echo's instant counter,
        a sinuate lessening. Jazz trumpet
    in the bridge! Elbows up through a pop song,

        I'm off on / the wrong step, listening to
        my life.

ONE CHILLY NIGHT IN MY EMPTY CHILDHOOD HOME

Horizontal, alone with the ceiling stucco.
    Plus ça change: a neural portal
    unlatched by wind's falsetto:
    that pimentoless olive-green door
at 392 Friendship Avenue.

Family & furniture out, before new owners, I kip
    over one spring night on pastel carpet
as if a poet, attending, as the house

    divests itself.
    Some point was to be made.

A plenipotentiary yet / weighs down
    the fibres, casts to headwinds
    a golden-eyed kestrel
to wait out the shadowmouse.

MY CRYING AT WORK IS OF FRUSTRATION AND HOPELESSNESS

Mind & body to opposite corners
    of the ring. Two surgeries, six years,
and my knee's never

    not been swollen. I now know commodity:
        degenerative drag: a rootedness
        that ivies being as I scope each here
    to deadeye the easily accessed chair.

My thirties dwindle to
    one lunch hour, the greige quiet room off
Invesco's cafeteria. Ingrown & out-turned

    has birthed
        the centripetal. I've become
        who I am. God,
    love me.

1 A.M. WALK GETS HER IN TROUBLE FOR STAYING OUT

Aperture, wide: this pathway lamp
    the colour temperature of
a DIY incubator –

    I've kissed a girl before,
        kept my eyes open each time
    like a naturalist. But a gust insists on here:

        an hour plus we lean each to each
            mistaking satellite for star. Evening / chill.

Spores of her perfume on
    my one cool shirt: hair-trigger olfac-
    tory bombs. Continuity
issues in a long take exist, they just

    take longer to emerge.
    The night's light's inside out.

WHEN I WAS FOUR SHE WAS TWENTY-FIVE

Line: 'Do people get sick
    from kissing?' Knee-
    highs on Mom, faux leather, heels
    a square root. Pinched visual field:
the concrete walk of a strip mall:

    a portico to
    perspective's fall-off.

Top of boot, long stroke of
    pencil-brown hair. Cue her laugh.
    The spatiotemporal,
beakered for less than an instant,

    leaves a grey residue.
        Her no a variegated no that
    resolves to a / beautiful / marble.

HANGING AUGUST'S FULL-LENGTH BEDROOM MIRROR

The silver misfires. Fluorescence a ferret
    along my underlid: celestial miscue, flashes
of hope & starry tumble

    like swanning
        into the sun. A microsecond's
    suicide. An *and.*

Another saccade, another
    sack of sadness / dragged through dust.
    The light a squeeze of lemon juice
that ignites

    a paper cut. I must to the last
        while the retinue of trapezists
        reassembles
    my reflected gasp.

Mission Architecture

Like a boat floating above its shadow
Build here the soul of thread

— LISA ROBERTSON

Hexagonal Prism
Piano Wire
Keeping It Simple

The room in which I sit is a hexagonal prism: a hexagonal floor and ceiling, six symmetrical walls with one door for ingress and egress. The door is an unidentifiable silver alloy strangely warm to the touch, deadening the occasional outer vocal exhortation, mechanical moan or febrile whine. This is not a dream but it is dreamlike, which I've come to know as consonant. In time there's more time, one creates time by anticipating its lengthening and expecting its end, though this is the same everywhere, isn't it, yes it is. Sunlight's absent from the room, one window high on the wall opposite suggests I am inground, perhaps this room nests within another, within another still, so on and so on, I am the pith. I will keep this simple to begin. A wooden chair, not uncomfortable. A table. Upon the table a recording device, voice-activated, *dasZeug* emblazoned on its face, my compatriot and commensal, whose microphone grille is the bars of a cage, is sewer grate to the tunnel to the causeway to the mud-slick hand clawing earth under a swept field where the horizon stretches piano wire to constituents and the sky shaves off nanos of blue to ripple around my feet. I will keep this simple. The microphone protrudes from the audio interface, mounted on the end of an industrial metal appendage.

This is more than a recording device, more than vibrations into syllables into words, words into codec into alphanumeric lines that traffic the telescreen hoisted by the mechanical arm aslant from the housing case. The Coats point to it, utter *tsoyk, das tsoyk*, they diligently monitor my lapses, demanding each thought vocalized. They do not understand that sometimes truth surfaces like a haunted face in knotted oak under irreducible qualities of shadow and mood and memory. Yet it is my appointed task to quicken. To incite. There is everything to remember and so little that remains and naught but wave packets ghosting the boundary condition. The Coats have waited years for the morphology to align so that my message has a hope of consummation. I will keep it simple. You are me, I am you, and of the things I am compelled to articulate foremost among them is this.

The Subject Sighs
A Structure from Nowhere
Explain Fear

I am not a clone. I am not a doppelgänger or a multiversal self parting the curtain on continuum. I've seen all the shows you have, read the books you have, your reference points are my reference points and I'm not among them. It's imposture to claim otherwise. The subject sighs, thought to ego, ego to act. When I say 'I,' you must conjure a heliotropic flowerhead, a hand held to the sun, 'I' am the glow of skin under incandescent light, the freefall of associative memory triggered by a wayward breeze. 'You' are the surety of proprioception, the pitch and tone of inner voice that intimates 'here,' the circle plane over the square. The scene in which the hero shaves his head and stares at the bathroom mirror, don't look for me in the reflection but in the recognition, the reflected gasp. If you are to make progress at all, if you are to scorch the transmission between a thought had and a thought compelled, you must escape your own room, your own hexagonal prism with silver door. Let me illuminate by parse_error_10 plain, or desert's logical endpoint, salt flats that elude geolocation. No bioforms, no vegetal presence, no motility whatsoever, hard-baked carmine sand nearly glass, horizons unyielding in every direction with your lone figure to mark dimension. Beside you a structure, as if fallen from nowhere, from a colossal box of jacks. What does it mean to loom? It's motion without motion, or unregistered motion, and that's what the structure does, it looms: springcreak, cross-hatched rebar of unknown origin and function with blades configured on the silica for pinpoint load-bearing capacity. There are many of these jacks, constellated, spaced far enough apart to frustrate comprehension of their pattern. In later years the closest you come to explaining the sensation is keno-phobia, your recurring dream as a child on Penn Avenue while your baby brother slept and cried and slept and grew. Explain fear, dear brother, padded in your crib with arms thrust up.

A Letter
Chemical Romance
'What I Know I Believe'

A letter arrives, cursive on the envelope familiar but slippery, stygian ink weighting the ascenders and descenders with a touch of January night over Lake Huron, its amethyst like a flicker in aquarium glass. You kick through two feet of snow to shorebound ice to spell MATT + KIM in giant letters while she stands behind you, barely recognizable under the layers of down and wool, shrinking with the perspective as you move to her 'M'. Snowflakes begin as strange attractors. You open the letter or you don't open the letter. It rests on the shelf in your vestibule among the keys and coins as the day dilates and the quotidian rushes in, pools around your feet, the grey-and-beige muck. How many origin stories has pop culture imagined for you: frigates in the atmosphere gunning through methane and sulphur, the chemical romance between microbes, sudden thermal imbalance generating a life force. Augie, when he's compelled to tell you something, rarely fails to address you first. 'Dada,' he says and waits for acknowledgement, are all children like this? How long parse_error_0 longer. 'Yes?' 'Dada, nobody at school believes I'm a ninja.' Etc. You don't open the letter. 'What I know I believe,' merely a cue from Wittgenstein that chitters in your head as you dog your son up the stairs to brush his teeth for bed. Parenting requires a magician's misdirection, not just to distract from hurts and aches or tantrums and boredom but to smooth the acceleration through cognition, explications that don't confuse but satisfy, the arm-wearying wave of orange paddles at unstoppable incoming freight. I believe you do open the letter and read words I've spoken here inside my room, a reassurance that parallel lives, yes, can converge. Ah, the letter as object has no purchase, no wave is alike and yet they're the same, repetition with variation along the shoreline. Augie at five months. Charmaine holds him by his arms to plant his curled toes in the cold Great Lake tide. The current he gathers inside himself becomes a wail.

Versal Deformations
We, You, Me
Betta Fish

A frisson among the Coats before today's session, from cinder and scatter the homeward flow of data has made the experiment a qualified success. The membrane is permeable, through versal deforms parse_error_01 the 6-gon field, say the Coats. I have for moments felt a spectral weight, heard a diapason-like waterfall through pores in the concrete walls. As if slowly crushed by decoherence, as if assuming number like a character in Yvegeny Zamyatin's *We*: you/me shall wilt before the end. Take whatever solace or relief you can before the uploading, imma-nence like a lighthouse, its flicker-flicker-sweep over dark seams roughing the surface of the harbour. 'Don't multiply entities beyond necessity' goes Occam's razor, an apposite lyric for the melody we're hearing, wouldn't you say. If only this were as easy as microfiche smuggled across the border. It is not infor-mation I must pass on but knowledge, which becomes knowledge only if someone experiences it, maps it and marks its place under the everyday, locked and chained and ready to be unearthed by the spade tip. The worst day in Augie's life, he says, was the day he buried in the garden bed the betta fish he routinely failed to feed. Ah, lived irony cuts through penitential bloat. You remember Kierkegaard, who claims that the capacity for, the openness to, the uncanny leads to a more authentic existence. Are you hearing this trickle? Pretense falls away and reveals a void so resounding the echo is more material than its container, is irony 'all the way down,' the feel of inclined curve at high speed, the tug of g as determined by a / $\sin \theta$, the flight impulse in a grounded creature divided by time left on earth.

Full-Body Sigh
Brute Fact
An Invisible Someone

Early weeks, and Charmaine and you take turns at skin-to-skin time with August. Memories you're unsure have happened nevertheless maintain presence, as when that gust of wind, where was it, you were a teenager, picked up brittle fallen leaves on a late October day and spun a hollow cylinder around you as its centre, what were the chances. Pressing August into your bare chest, you take the stairs to the basement couch and he full-body sighs into you, into nowhere else. Regulation of heartbeat, of breath, in proportion to my allotted. The anthropic principle reasons that humans see the physical universe as is because how else could it appear, the values of electromagnetic force or Z-boson mass or Boltzmann constant that allow life to evolve shouldn't surprise us with their precision because we are here to witness them. If they were otherwise, we simply would not be. The sludge of night cages an auroral flicker: spliced frames of spent anguish, blankets curled and twisted around your nineteen-year-old self when God was the simplest explanation for the why. Your ex, seven years your senior and after the briefest of relationships, went ahead with the abortion you chokingly told her you couldn't pay for, you were Catholic, relying on her decision-making to keep your conscience and to conserve your life's path. Isn't He always the brutish of brute facts. No matter how infinitesimal the knot becomes, there are more causal loops that parse_error_1 Regret can have positive value as well as negative, it can cool the counterfactuals until excitation dissipates at the xanthic endpoint of Kelvin, the copper dust suspended like faith. 'The splinter in your eye is the best magnifying glass,' says Adorno, are you the eye and I the splinter? Eight years after August's sigh conferred heartsease, he tells you about an invisible someone who he feels is watching him all the time, at school, at home, except when he's playing with friends. What you didn't say: 'The someone is you, August.'

Yellowjacket
A Four-Year-Old's Stoicism
Up-Gathering Pitch

The yellowjacket caught inside the kitchen stitches a succession of escape attempts, each ending at the sliding-door pane with the sound of a needle-bar stroke. It projects panic but surely can't be panicked, it's acting reasonably if reason were mere application of non-heuristic algorithm, an automaton whose behaviour is a function of intent not result. In the kitchen you and the wasp are two beings whose contemporaneity charges the 3-space, a vitalism almost electrostatic, a thousand eyes glittering. You sidle toward the door, slide it open and wait. Between us there is but this. On the first day of kindergarten Augie was stung on his hand by a bee, we always say 'bee' though it was likely a wasp, and remarkably he didn't cry. Unexpected stoicism from a four-year-old to match the momentous day. He often asks for that story about you at his age, where a rumble of fellow kindergartners approach you in your place under the far-corner tree, ask what you're doing there alone and you deadpan, 'Just watching a bee fly around my head.' Played for laughs four decades later but you remember it as your first attempt at agency, as though individualism must be palpable to others. The physicist Julian Barbour claims that past and future are merely places, we exist in them as people exist in separate places across the globe, the country, a neighbourhood. To hold in mind compossible paths: I am that kid under the tree, you are that kid, Augie is in the principal's office with a sore pinky, is struggling to raise his head during tummy time on the couch, is snipping the hose with pruning shears, is exerting pressure on imagination's up-gathering pitch. Is in the car seat: 'Dada?' 'Yes?' 'I keep thinking about stuff-I-like dying, I can't stop, I just try to put it out of my mind.' It's not that the wasp notices it's cleared the pane, darting error-free, unimpeded into and beyond the backyard. Nor is it in any sense back on track because in trying to escape it was already on track. It's the same creature displaced, processing as always the sensory cues, the instantiations of photon and turbulence and pheromone. There is nothing different in the wasp. There is something different about the wasp.

Haecceity
King's Corner and Hopscotch
The Present Ruin

The locus of difference is a static implosion, a fury, it's what Duns Scotus would call 'haecceity,' and it's the true vehicle of apprehension. You understand what I'm saying. Even subjects identical in every respect possess a 'thisness' which makes individual identity possible. Nothing lies like a grid. What makes you you emerges from your features and measurements or, further, flesh, bone, protein, cytoplasm, nuclei, gene, DNA, molecule, atom, proton, electron, quark. Pressure as parse_error_001 assemblage, scattered over an oil-stained floor waiting for the hobbyist mechanic to return, the interval ever-expanding. Determinism is product, Matthew Tierney your mechanism. You walk around the school where you once played, not your school but the one opposite your childhood home, you've only ever known it from the outside: red brick and barred windows, King's Corner and hopscotch squares, the tar-and-gravel roof when you rescued a tennis ball. Fact is tremulous the way metaphor is. Back when it was rundown, it's rundown now, the concrete around the grounds was fissured with grass and weeds, the basketball court an exercise in fantasy world-making, scarred islands, declensions in grey, tributaries toward a sea along the edge of the known. The present ruin is evocative, though the ruin must be of a different cycle, mustn't it, a sequence that began with late-summer peregrinations continues forty years later as cloud cover becomes a shield, a hull overturned, the air parse_error_10 The offset stutters and flowers, not unpleasant, not sustainable. No property differentiates one carbon molecule from another, you are swappable soma, what you know as your foot, your nose, your fingernails loses meaning at some level in the zoom. Atom, proton, electron, quark. We are made of effort. To be explicit, the ontotopology of negation is nonlinear when you consider, please consider, the quantum.

Mildly Bored Under Jupiter
Pivot
Gold Bars

In the Kawarthas you stand under the summer night sky, mildly bored, flashing back to your bedroom wall in grade school with its laminated star map. You wonder parse_error_1 to count as admiration, you're certain that yellow-bright one is Venus though later you find out, no, Jupiter. A star flickers, its light in past a speck, luminous flux in direct proportion to the thousands of photons that strike your retina. When light dims it seems to do so gradually, that is how we read the sensory data, but as the gap between photons increases it does not 'thin evenly,' does not fade on a continuum but in discrete levels reaching a denominator of brightness, like a stuck volume knob. A soap bubble, about to pop. The star flickers out and transmitters from the optic nerve zap your language centre, the projector coughs, the celluloid ticks, the white screen flickers in the slipstream of gelatin. Pivot: lab tables, fibre-optic cables and devices strewn as if all used up, safety earmuffs, goggles, crinkled Doritos bags and a raft of Coke cans, as a teenager you toured St. George Campus to construct a future and the future was physics, your projections a thought experiment on thought, like those photons lasered through parallel slits in two successive opaque plates to strike a third. What pattern on this third plate, what glimpse of intruder on the top landing, what shape discerned inside the spring fog, what faith wrenched from a godless world? Gold bars, pressed gold bars on the third plate, prove that light interferes with itself, acts as both wave and particle. Particles travel in a straight line, Augie can hide around a corner and whack you with the pillow he calls 'Bijou' because you can't see around corners, can you. Yet fire one photon at a time, picture each *phtting* from a finger gun, what could that single photon possibly interfere with? Nothing. But still, light fans into the gold bars of interference as if the photons had arrived at the plate simultaneously. They didn't, they did. An Elsinorian pall darkens the face of Niels Bohr in his Copenhagen study. The pattern is the same. The photon takes both paths, the architectonic brain disintegrates.

Attenuation
Proof of Concept
The Mountain Trembles

The genuine attenuation in Augie's voice: 'It's sad when people lose people.' Watching Marlon Brando as Jor-El address Clark Kent holographically at the inception of the Fortress of Solitude, downwelling light in the crystal cave a world's-edge blue. What sequence of occurrences like chord progressions might unlock the phrasing and harmonic colour of August's character such that you might look back and say this, there, that was him, or looking forward to the adult you will never fully know: that is who he is. Your son. We flee into entirety, viaducts of alternate choices, without an outside perspective. The error is in thinking that Nietzsche killed God when he merely announced He was dead, says Marcus Steinweg, clarifying further that to believe in God you must first kill Him. You must point yourself like a gun. Look around the room, take as 'room' a broader sense of place and place as point of communion with curvature. Apprehend non-being. Do you shed dimensions one by one by one, does thisness tunnel through you? The 'I' can be many things: a metaphysical error, says Carlo Rovelli, a claim on the universe, says Weil, a proof of concept, says the primary investigator, her coat blanking out my peripheral vision. I lean midriff into table, imbalance flaring on unlevel chair legs while you stare at white pixels, search for resistance, the nodes between phenomena. Ah, it comes, the way a poem comes, in time: *dasZeug* emits a low-intensity chirp, scrambling the Coats, a chirp hither like a throwaway from cosmic noon. Intent finds its mirror. The mountain trembles as we brandish a wooden sword and remake in our own image He who made us in His. Angular CGI ice in Superman's retreat explodes upward, so too Augie's newfound realization of one death ahead of another's, which is an anything as good as nothing.

Nitrile Blue
A Place Clean of Wrong
Incompatibilism

When Charmaine in her early forties got pregnant without 'trying' or even a thought to trying, she didn't know until past caring, a heavier bleed, a curiosity, an outtake before your one and only son like a scherzando toddles back in. 'We did it by ourselves, I knew we could do it,' Charmaine said at the time, smiling. Two years later, again pregnant, again without the daily syringe of gonadotropin, superovulation, ultrasounds and pinched mornings at Mount Sinai, without the black spheroid pills of traditional Chinese medicine, without endometrial scraping and sippy cups, stolid airport hue of post-surgery lounge, two rows of reclining women, couples occupying the thinnest of effervescent layers just then hit by the sun, an anechoic chamber whose hush is heroic, without intracytoplasmic sperm injection, without monitored uterine lining, blastocyst grades, familiarity and hunger, nitrile blue hands busy in the sliver of lab window, hope muffled by nature's embrace, or is it Nature's, is it snowing or is it springtime that third and last-chance IVF. By then the file folder towered, no explanation for the infertility, every box checked. What it's like to fall to one's death in a place clean of wrong: you fall forever, die and decompose in flight, tattered clothes flapping in a fist-blown whistle, drywell wail. The brain is relational, notices with increasing regularity only difference, sits within not above as physics' Standard Model makes of things a thing worth striving for. From outside my prism a scuffling cough rises unannounced and emanates from the left wall, becomes as do these words coded and digitized, a charge of phenomena over the error floor. Here and there blinks like a cursor. During that second unheralded pregnancy, what enters at nervous laughter's zenith? A prodrome of incompatibilism, a few weeks' viability that teases Charmaine and you with a sibling for Augie before you succumb. Consciousness is consciousness of consciousness of love.

Sun on Oils
Yawn
Disconsolate Whinges

One of the Coats scrapes open the door at an off-hour and with it comes a whiff of dankness, of recess, cardboard sentinels amid moonlight, Granddad's canvases and tarps, your brothers and you bunking in the basement while plaster walls crack imperceptibly, like years. How you alone ran the half-acre in Marmora under no one's eye, the railroad track past the copse marking the exclusion zone, and though you had no wish to be elsewhere you dreamed elsewhere, lorded it over the insect world. It was sun on oils. I suppose you run by or through me as we both listen for the chirr of grasshoppers while in your hand a glass jar rhymes medium with spectrum. In rushes crescendo. 'Is it the sky that shudders,' I ask a Coat, who blinks rapidly, slams shut the door, *dasZeug* a lotus flower, stealing my breath. Our lives shuffle from one container to the next with rare moments of disclosure when we're thrown clear of the present's abyss. Here's a memory: a man sitting in front of you on the bus, the back of his neck pitted, and when he nods forward the pits 'yawned open' you say afterward to a friend whose admixture of disgust and mirth is a preservative. What is this place where words become matter, where numbers wink, deep-set in nightfelt. I realize what I could make disappear were I only to try: the lights, the table, the Coat on hands and knees tapping the wall. The wall. 'It is difficult to begin at the beginning': Wittgenstein again, and parse_error_00 crouching, the duration of a chirp, it's working says a Coat as I cling to disconsolate whinges in *dasZeug* to resituate me, re-erect the hexagonal walls, the savanna, the dupable praying mantis that decapitates a grasshopper then polishes its head as if sanding a gemstone. The glass jar a contact relic, you turn and face the last of me. A decaying note asks of itself its origins in a material universe. The wind rustles the yellow-brown August stalks.

The Three-Body Problem
Kepler's Ellipses
I Fire a Harpoon

No formula can predict the orbital motions of three celestial masses acted upon only by mutual attraction. The three-body problem: you and Charmaine and August in the hours before he was born, flint colliding with stone, a Zeusian peal, the random bounce of persons like gas particles defining the cuboids of cafeteria, glass elevator, bathroom, waiting room, and on, and on. Hewing to the orthogonal, Charmaine and you dutifully follow the labyrinth that offered up no decisions for long stretches unless sleeplessness and hindsight made them appear as such. Whosoever is is on autopilot, the way I stumble now through the compound's wreckage and ash terrain without leaving my wooden not-uncomfortable chair. From plummet to peace all of us twist in time. He is tiny, 5 lbs., 8 oz., Tummy Mummy had been forty-eight hours in labour plus another hour in the hospital room with her mother and brother and August, August Charles, August Charles Tierney. That hour a black box, a magnetic moment, an elsewise that fans out with mercurial phrasing and reaches Charmaine and you in the small, private waiting room, a red LED clock high on the wall. A situation is a fundamental privation of being, a lack: were being a sound wave it would contain echo's instant counter in every place not-you. Resistance reduces to every felt thing. Before Kepler, orbits were circles, the circle was Platonic, and music triumphed. Kepler's ellipses, with their two foci, one for the sun and another for the emptiness facing the sun, do not happen without Tycho Brahe and his astronomical instruments, a lifetime of tracings and x-ings and noted observations. My mind is evaporating, I fire a harpoon at the bank of stars. You have escaped your hexagonal room and the counterturning begins, the thread catching on August's birthdate, the provincial Family Day, as the polar vortex moves in.

11

STRANDED ON THE JUNGLE GYM AFTER MORNING BELL IN KINDERGARTEN

Tossed by an east wind
    atop marrowless metal shafts:
viaducts of alternate choices:

    I stand as I.
        Nonplussed. The drop off
        the implausibly high fireman's pole / a gulp
    of witches' brew, bittersweet. *You got*

        up there …!, the teacher yells,
            birthing ellipses that will
            forevermore marshal
        my attempts at ready existence.

The rest of the class a stretching cat
    before homeroom doors, my inmost
bursts, trickles down recesses.

A SPARSELY ATTENDED RAVE IN 1989

A tower speaker the monolith
    negating prosaic dimensions, 'Bizarre
Love Triangle' is

    the configuration it tasks those on the ware-
        house floor in Pickering or is it
    Ajax, Ontario. *Far*

    smash cut to *away*, New Order
        deconceptualizes
        Gaussian functions, unstacks the
        block universe: bedrock to geodesy:
    frieze to orientation: object to being.

A higher purpose lassos our dance moves
    leaving halos of dry ice. At once
I perceive the too few in the few.

THE MASS WHERE I MISS THE DAYS OF UNADULTERATED BELIEF

Process is active faith.
    Sunday like the Lady of the Lake,
    phosphorescent before
the foundling, such vulgar hope. / Most church

    days a frothing wake,
        all shellacked grain that ends
        in the same hard place: my son
        running Hot Rods over the crimson-
    cushioned kneeler.

In chimerical colours
at water's edge, the 'noble lie'

    is God and a child.
        He & he
    brandish a wooden sword.

RUMOUR HAS IT HE THINKS I 'STOLE' HIS GIRLFRIEND

Aswim in Boehner's suit, bowtie cocked:
    downtown Sheraton, 'Forever Young' for the night:
she & I have not / yet

    quite – stalactite to stalagmite –

        I look to be fucked: the ex and his posse
           barred by hotel security atop
        the down escalator.

Is pretense of courage / courage? O Socrates,
would that I did not know myself.

Chatter like oakum
    insulates my unease. Synth horns advance
    a proposition for the future: accept risks of
    out-purpling your boutonniere / to be
the moral character.

AFTER SCHOOL MY FRIEND'S MOM SPEAKS HER MIND

I don't want him here! She said it, hidden.
    I enter the kitchen: a Brady's off-off-white,
    oatmeal & cream, camel hump.
I heard (hear it still), eyeballing

    Mark's mom as gauzy mom-smear:
        curlers, stay-at-home ferocity.
        Limbs and joints in the moment
    Meccano-sized, my body / I realize

        a transaction bartered these six years
            with others, beggared by hurtfelt.
        No apology – else apology never arrived at.

Alpha & beta,
    we circle snarling and the circle is the
resolution, tundra to our backs.

FIRST-PERIOD GEOGRAPHY I SAT BEHIND LISA SEIDER

Filmstrip feed & take-up reel
    like two crows perched. A kid with cheater's grin
    licks an ice cream
in a black & white Siberia deep

    with days undreamt. Milk solid, shaped by
      its bucket at minus some degrees Celsius
      and what does she / Lisa / say, sidelong in
    the slipstream of gelatin & fluorescence?

My buck teeth never
    as remarkable or severe, my high school crush
    refers to the Russian mother & father
as 'us,' catches herself, an aliquot

    of embarrassment that sustains the half
    of it.

SCORING AT WILL WHILE PLAYING SHINNY ON THE RIVER

How long those two toughs tried to catch me.
    Because the goals had come easy? Or
    as leporine, forsaken, thinkery
was I sufficient condition? My glee

    for show (a brother, plus the McCowans),
        stalks & reeds like
        landmine collateral
    mid-blast. By reckon

        of dilating sun, I tendered myself,
        I couldn't see going on. / Caged helmet

        smashed into a Rouge
            that used to freeze: *Let it come,*
            I remember thinking, watching myself
        skate away.

THE CEILING FAN ON A SLEEPLESS SNOWY NIGHT

A mobile, immobile: blades at the mercy
    of fluid dynamics,
its mercurial phrasing.

Tick tock, root rot. Schist / shift.
    Yttriferous-slick sleeplessness
    proves the heart's a revenant.
Ain't it. My mattress

    the buttress against updrafts
        of temporal drift. Before bed
        I'd read (before retucking in my son)
    an email from Tummy Mummy: her love

        of snow. Morning comes a superhero.
            Daylight saving's gilt stillness.
        Boots crunch past. Radio static, window.

WAS IT ART CLASS OR RELIGION AT ST. BRENDAN'S?

A carved soap boat, Ivory,
afloat in the surround:

a memory flare, as if *ex nihilo*.
Within one's timeline,
collective industry
of flux, radiation, molecule
reduces to every felt thing. / Frailest,

the snowflakes fall.
Such harmlessness present!
Dispersive noise

in the signal – white to pink – almost
defogs into pure stream. A moment
amphibian, with weak heart,

darts error-free.

THE PSYCHEDELIC FURS THROUGH MONUMENT VALLEY SILENCE

On course.
    'The Ghost in You' on MP3, nanites
    assemble an emotional corollary.
    Crimson steppe of Navajo territory
a new-to-us palette

    that fastens flat earth,
        realigns momentum, white line, release.
    Determinism is / product.

I have before, will again, pinch your belly, empty
the syringe of gonadotropin.

Our top secret, subcutaneous.
    Love remains blameless, the screen door
you fail to see until

    you run through it. Next stop: Los Alamos.

AT THE BEACH I SURPRISE US BOTH WITH A PROPOSAL

Still harbouring next door's chainsaw buzz
    (goodbye, copse between cottages)
    that chased us
from deck to beach this September weekend: *together*

    becomes merely sounds I'd / heard before.
        Blown vacuum chamber, wind like Zeus
        dropping by to whinge about the at-it-again
    mortals …

I peer not out of but around
    and inhabit *willyou?* Now / makes itself clear
to alternatives: this boulder we're perched on

    in the shallows: all arms and legs and élan,
        phlegmatic humour, *Dasein*, Parmendian One,
    Great Lake tide & phlogiston.

ON THE ROOF OF SCARBOROUGH CAMPUS U OF T, 3 A.M.

Mastodon rumble of
    observatory dome, slo-mo swivel.
    With a series of glottal stops
    the sixty-inch-lens telescope
clicks inputted coordinates into place.

Where pathos / approximates grace, minutes
    fold-tuck B into A
under the stellar narrows. No

    more did I hold Jupiter's gaze
        than note the discharge of ions
    as Earth's rotation sped.

The transgression – in past, a speck –
    widens in time
out of proportion to my allotted.

POP MUSIC COMES TO LINEATE THE SCHOOL YEARS

Kids from the neighbourhood
    are faceless even in the moment
of recognition. Skateboard / skateboard

    over new asphalt, on median incline
        to a basketball court overtaken
    by line infantry of weeds.

'Hold Me Now' mingles with mortar-
    grey isotopes that've escaped
to decay freely into dusk.

I am
too far in it to get out / but

    tread the cusp, girls & boys,
        longing almost sentient,
    a meanwhile before the mighty sun.

PLAYING SOFTBALL WITH HER CHURCH GROUP

One's first love is whole-
    sale, amethyst, a cluster of galaxies
in red shift. An offshoot in

    the natural arc: that summer's end-of-week co-ed
        slow-pitch game
    amongst fundamentalists.

Mostly lapsed, I mostly
played shortstop. Felt

    I had nothing to add. Feel still.
        She, nightly, destabilized what belief spins,
    incommensurable as the cross,

    the sword. Details like Ronnie's spikes-high slide,
        communal pregame prayer, grasslick
    have no place. Snow has fallen since.

DOWNCAST AT SEVEN YEARS OLD ON OUR OLD STREET

Brow coldshaping a coin on car window
    approaching Penn Avenue / and *om*
    goes the engine, skyrift opening
my known & manufactured

background. Fact is I, I, I, inserting
    presence into 'a last look' at home.
    Conscious of melancholy, acting
like a first-timer, I kite

    the charge of phenomena
    over the error floor.

A Moog synth thrums my core,
    reassurance
    that parallel lives, yes, can
converge.

WEEKENDS STITCH TOGETHER A LONG-DISTANCE RELATIONSHIP

Monday, 5 a.m. neardark: frosty campus:
   cross-sectioned paths,
      node after node flooded
      by halogen, precarity.
   Ascent *sans* height, each circle of lamplight
a bath in essence of canary

   toward the T.O.-bound Greyhound &
   my morning class.

Among the briefcases of Guelphites
   who bear life decisions in
aggregate, my duffel bag of sour laundry.

Our silence is exponential,
   hurtles south into QEW traffic, sunrise,
simultaneity.

GAME OVER WHEN YOU TAKE THREE DIRECT HITS

Alone after long Tokyo months. Like Velcro
    ripped then reset, my weekly run to
Nakano for internet & inbox, galley café.

Afterward, I make my way
    to that first-person shooter, Mould's
    'Egøverride' leaking from earbuds
into station-adjacent arcade.

From cinder & scatter the
    homeward flow. Significant,
I bury my sight into act & potency. / The crosshairs

    obey, built-in lag
    coded by its makers. Gamification

      renews the steep.
      All my knowns become knew.

FALL TERM IN GRADE 6 I SAT BESIDE PAUL BIGIONI

A crack in affinity. / I wiggled, shed months of being
    popular, asked Ms. Grishko,
    Can I move from the back?
feigning trouble with the chalkboard.

Columnar seating plan like
legionnaires marching on the capitol.

Decamped, flush with
    decisiveness, I understand the in-crowd
    is supersaturated, that water bugs
    flee on surface tension:
phenomena real-world, wild, cool.

All eyes drift to curriculum
    while the offset stutters & flowers
as kaleidoscope. School, once.

Abandoned cowfield uphill
    from cottage rentals. Agglutinates
    in the brushwork thicken the episode
    to agency & evolution, threat, sun, scale, tim-
ber fence, spasm, mask, debt.

Not / not wanting to …
    Absent any idea beyond what emerged
    dumbfounded from the cave
    of the other: younger cousin, brother.
Like the roaming bull that rumour

    conjured. We bring creation to a small-
    mouth bass, chucking stones to shock it

      off an altar. A stickiness in the mechanism.
      Taking turns. Ever heavier rocks.

AS DALE HARDING IN 'ONE FLEW OVER THE CUCKOO'S NEST,' I HAVE A BREAKDOWN

The fogroll of attention, 200 stilled faces
    sheared by shadow. Slumped to knees
        I adjudge the heft
        of speech, each emotive rattle
    a transgression on failsafe. Not once able
to call forth tears, as if

    I had within / a proscenium arch,
        observing myself near the stage lip
        draw the foolproof spot and / like Euclid
    test its axioms.

Black paint layers the risers, covering
    past productions,
    and I extend my gaze
into it, rest my head, before the lifting of.

THE U.S. SOUTHWEST, AFTER A MISCARRIAGE

Wind, over alkali flats. Wind through
    brambles, tufts, hi-hats,
    ground-down stuff. Mint-green
lizard with a thousand eyes / glittering

    on its back. Every hollow owns
    a sound: fist-blown whistle, drywell wail.

Into what / the least path leads,
    rented Nissan hiding from view
    us two, immutable,
head resting on a shoulder.

In the cradle, conditions for admission. What
we want, to want to stop.

The ball-bearing must roll.
Sand-shapes form a parabola.

THE LAST NEW YEAR'S EVE I'M FORCED TO SPEND WITH FAMILY

Over the lip into an era of
    projection, my inner warlock a figure
    of billow, of twitch. Sony Walkman
    a dimensional hatch as 'Every Little Thing ... '
ticks to 'Invisible Sun' ...

The minivan's back row
    affords a wide-angle view
of four brothers dozing: incoming January

    shades parents, the outland parting
    for rumble-grey bumper. Missing the big party –

    starburst on a soap bubble –

      my upset foams and dissolves
        into a downflow
      channelled by rhythm.

Purchased for the boy I wasn't,
    frame unfrozen by time, a lickety-splitty
    three-speed with wingspan
of a pterodactyl: Dad heffalumping

    downfield in unzipped galoshes,
    a hand under seat rim. Springmelt

        mirrors clouds
            on the track oval, underscores the
            sensation of velocity. Attempts / mount.
        Dad lets go with no word.

Oblivious, I ride
    over the earth's ribs: each foot
    at six o'clock lifts off / its pedal. Upright!
Proof a force spent madly in flight.

I PASS HIS SCHOOL DURING LUNCH

Playground a-squawk. From the southside
    street opposite / out for a daytime walk
        I first spot his jacket. Like a binary star
        my son rising pixelated on
    the far horizon: those bits I own
as atmosphere to my core.

He continues to / not see me, tuned
    to other kids, scoring diacritics
        on the utility pole. What is, emptying
what was: the edifice I know

    as lent, soul temporal, inscribing
        duration, the middle of the end.
    Whether or not I walk on, I do

        and I don't. When I go, he'll be gone.

Sonnetlog

Changelog

// Hexagonal Prism / Piano Wire / Keeping It Simple: –

// The Subject Sighs / A Structure from Nowhere / Explain
Fear: 24, 34, 20

// A Letter / Chemical Romance / 'What I Know I Believe':
76, 31, 19, 77, 73

// Versal Deformations / We, You, Me / Betta Fish: 79, 15, 26

// Full-Body Sigh / Brute Fact / An Invisible Someone: 74,
18, 17

// Yellowjacket / A Four-Year-Old's Stoicism / Up-Gathering
Pitch: 83, 11, 71

// Haecceity / King's Corner and Hopscotch / The Present
Ruin: 16, 72, 80, 21

// Mildly Bored Under Jupiter / Pivot / Gold Bars: 74, 84, 68,
14, 15

// Attenuation / Proof of Concept / The Mountain Trembles:
27, 63, 65

// Nitrile Blue / A Place Clean of Wrong / Incompatibilism:
72, 83, 77

// Sun on Oils / Yawn / Disconsolate Whinges: 13, 23, 12

// The Three-Body Problem / Kepler's Ellipses / I Fire a
Harpoon: 24, 70, 29, 71

Devlog

// Opening epigraph from 'Sing a Darkness', *Then the War*, Carl Phillips, Farrar, Straus and Giroux, 2022.

// 'We Are Told There Is No Longer a Heartbeat': 'Intake & sorrow' from 'By Torchlight Through a Ventilation Brick', *Swivelmount*, Ken Babstock, Coach House Books, 2020.

// 'Mission Architecture' epigraph from 'The Present', *R's Boat*, Lisa Robertson, University of California Press, 2010.

// 'Nitrile Blue / A Place Clean of Wrong / Incompatibilism':

    1 From Plotinus, *Enneads* VI.9.9: 'Here is the soul's peace, outside of evil, refuge taken in the place clean of wrong'

   10 From Jorge Luis Borges, 'The Library of Babel', translated by Andrew Hurley: 'I am preparing to die, a few leagues from the hexagon where I was born. When I am dead, compassionate hands will throw me over the railing; my tomb will be the unfathomable air, my body will sink for ages, and will decay and dissolve in the wind engendered by my fall, which shall be infinite.'

// 'Downcast at Seven Years Old on Our Old Street': 'And Om' from the album *Graz*, Nils Frahm, Erased Tapes, 2021.

// 'Was It Art Class or Religion at St. Brendan's?': 'Path 19 (yet frailest)' from the album *From Sleep*, Max Richter, Deutsche Grammophon, 2015.

// 'Error Key' lines from 'Variations on No Theme', *Ashes for Breakfast: Selected Poems*, Durs Grünbein, translated by Michael Hofmann, Farrar, Straus Giroux, 2005.

// Poems from this manuscript have previously appeared in *The Fiddlehead*, *Juniper Poetry*, and *The Walrus*.

// The Canada Council for the Arts and the Ontario Arts Council provided funding to write the poems.

// Thanks to Alana Wilcox, Crystal Sikma, James Lindsay, and everyone at Coach House Books for their support and belief in the book. Thanks to Laura Brown for lending me her photographic eye, and Professor Li Qian for time in her photonics lab. Thanks to Steve McOrmond, first reader, sounding board, and comrade. Thanks to my editor, the brainiac Karen Solie, for dragging these poems into the light.

// Thanks to Charmaine for allowing me (as always) to write openly about our life together, for her careful edits, and for shouldering the load when I was off poem-making. Bottomless love to her and to August, my problem solvers.

Error Key

Every crack is a missing piece,
And the effort of finding it is a psalm.

Matthew Tierney is the author of four previous books of poetry, most recently *Midday at the Super-Kamiokande*. He won the 2013 Trillium Book Award for Poetry and is also a recipient of the K. M. Hunter Award and the P. K. Page Founders' Award. He works for U of T as a writer in the Faculty of Applied Science & Engineering and lives in the east end of Toronto.

Typeset in Warnock and DIN Next Pro.

Printed at the Coach House on bpNichol Lane in Toronto, Ontario, on Zephyr Antique Laid paper, which was manufactured, acid-free, in Saint-Jérôme, Quebec, from second-growth forests. This book was printed with vegetable-based ink on a 1973 Heidelberg KORD offset litho press. Its pages were folded on a Baumfolder, gathered by hand, bound on a Sulby Auto-Minabinda, and trimmed on a Polar single-knife cutter.

Coach House is on the traditional territory of many nations, including the Mississaugas of the Credit, the Anishnabeg, the Chippewa, the Haude-nosaunee, and the Wendat peoples, and is now home to many diverse First Nations, Inuit, and Métis peoples. We acknowledge that Toronto is covered by Treaty 13 with the Mississaugas of the Credit. We are grateful to live and work on this land.

Edited by Karen Solie
Cover design by Crystal Sikma, cover artwork *RISES-5*, screenprint on
    paper, 2020, by Meaghan Hyckie
Interior design by Crystal Sikma
Author photo by Laura Brown

Coach House Books
80 bpNichol Lane
Toronto ON M5S 3J4
Canada

416 979 2217
800 367 6360

mail@chbooks.com
www.chbooks.com